SHELLEY ROTNER

Hello Spring!

Holiday House • New York

Winter.

Waiting . . .

for nature

to **wake up.**

Snowdrops peek out
from under melting snow.

The sun **shines** stronger.
The days get longer.
The earth warms.

Frozen streams thaw.
Tree sap flows.

A chorus of tree frogs sings wake up, wake up!

Crocuses tease,
bright yellow and purple,
promising warmer days to
come.

Buds **swell**.
Ferns **uncurl**.

Birds return with **song**,
busy building **nests**
and laying eggs.

Animals **wake up** from their deep winter sleep—
chipmunks, groundhogs, bats, bees, and bears.

Daffodils **dance**.
Dandelions **dot**.
Forsythia **shouts**!

Green is **growing** everywhere!

Hooray! Spring is here!

Baby animals are **born**—
chicks, kids, and piglets,
lambs, cubs, calves,
and colts.

Cherry blossoms pop and parade. Flowers bloom. It's a palette of petals.

You can **smell** that **spring** is in the air.

Pollen is carried from flower to flower. And then fruits and seeds can grow into new plants and trees.

It's the time to dig and plant.
Rain showers, seeds sprout,
gardens grow—
lettuce, beans, and peas.

Frogs **hop**.
Earthworms **creep**.
Turtles **crawl**.

Salamanders **emerge**.
Snakes **slither**.

Dragonflies **dart**.
Spiders **spin**.

Butterflies flit.
Bees buzz.
Ladybugs land.

Warm breezes **blow**.
Clouds float by.

The days get longer
and longer.

And **then** . . . it's the
longest day of the year,
and summer is here!

GLOSSARY

bud—a small plant part that grows into a flower, a leaf, or a branch

hibernation—spending the winter in an inactive state, sleeping or resting

kid—a young goat

pollen—the fine powder produced by flowers, needed to make fruit and seeds

pollination—the movement of pollen to parts deeper inside a flower so as to produce seeds and fruits

sap—the liquid inside a tree or other plant

spring equinox—the day in late March on which day and night are equal length or the same number of hours

summer solstice—the longest day of the year, or the day in late June that has the most sunlight hours

Dedicated to Mary Cash, my editor, who helps me reach my vision.

Special thanks to Dr. Linda Henderson, Diane deGroat, and designer Hans Teensma.

Printed and bound in September 2018 at Toppan Leefung, DongGuan City, China.
www.holidayhouse.com
10 9 8 7 6 5 4 3 2
Library of Congress Cataloging-in-Publication Data
Names: Rotner, Shelley.
Title: Hello spring! / Shelley Rotner.
Description: First edition. | New York : Holiday House, [2017] | Audience:
Age 4–8. | Audience: K to grade 3.
Identifiers: LCCN 2016032932 | ISBN 9780823437528 (hardcover)
Subjects: LCSH: Spring—Juvenile literature.
Classification: LCC QB637.5.R68 2017 |
DDC 508.2—dc23 LC record available at https://lccn.loc.gov/2016032932
ISBN 978-0-8234-3995-9 (paperback)